ELECTION!

ELECTION!

★ ★

A KID'S GUIDE TO PICKING OUR PRESIDENT

★ ★

Dan Gutman

Contents

* * *

Author's Note

* * *

It would have sounded awkward and repetitive to hear the words "the president" over and over again in this book. Because we haven't had a female president yet, it would have sounded even more awkward to refer to the president as "she" or "he/she." So within these pages, the president is sometimes referred to as "the president" and sometimes referred to as "he." No offense is intended to females, one of whom will surely be elected president of the United States sometime soon.

Introduction

★ ★ ★

Every four years, the grown-ups of America go a little crazy. You see grown men and women wearing funny hats and T-shirts, waving flags, putting goofy bumper stickers on their cars, buttons on their shirts, and signs on their front lawns. There are silly songs, slogans, ads, and balloons. It's like one big yearlong party.

In fact, what looks on the surface like craziness is actually very serious business. It is all part of the process of choosing the person who will lead the nation for the next four years.

When George Washington was elected in 1789, some people wanted to call him "His Highness," "His Elective Majesty," "His Supremacy," or "His Mightiness." In the end, they settled on a simpler, more down-to-earth title—the president of the United States.

Since Washington's time, the presidency has changed quite a bit and so has the process of electing a president, our nation's only nationally elected office. But one thing is constant. The decision about who will be president is one of the most important decisions that our country makes.

This year, you may be asking yourself what all the hoopla is about. A lot of questions may have popped into your head. *How powerful is the president? What happens if the president dies? What's the difference between a Democrat and a Republican? Can my mom or dad run for president? Do the candidates hate each other? How does a voting machine work? What can kids do to influence the election?*

The purpose of this book is to answer those questions (and about 120 more) in a simple and straightforward manner. Some of the answers may surprise you.

This book may not answer *every* question you have about the presidential election, but it will cover a lot of them. And it will give you a basic understanding of what all this national craziness is about.

ELECTION!

CHAPTER 1

★ ★ ★ ★ ★ ★ ★ ★ ★ ★ ★ ★ ★ ★ ★ ★ ★

The Presidency

Why do we have a president?

When the Revolutionary War ended in 1781 and America had won its independence from England, we didn't have a president. We didn't have a Constitution, either. At least not right away.

At first, the new nation was governed by Congress, which was a group of representatives from each of the thirteen original states. The problem was that each state had very different opinions about the way the country should be run.

There were arguments between states. At one point, Connecticut was claiming that it owned a large part of Pennsylvania.

It became clear that a stronger central government was needed to pull all the states together in a way that would be fair to all, big and small, north and south, rural and urban.

From May 25 through September 17, 1787, the "Founding Fathers" of our country gathered together at the old State House in Philadelphia. There, they wrote the Constitution, which is the foundation of our government. According to the Constitution, the executive branch of our government would be headed by a president. (For more about our government, see Chapter 2: Our Government.)

THE CONSTITUTION (Article II, Section I):
"The executive Power shall be vested in a President of the United States of America."

★

Who were the Founding Fathers?

They were fifty-five delegates from the twelve states (Rhode Island did not participate). Some were lawyers. Some were farmers. You may have heard some of their names before: George Washington, James

Madison, Benjamin Franklin. Thomas Jefferson was in Europe at the time.

★

What about the "Founding Mothers"?

In the 1700s, women were not believed to be capable of making important decisions. They did not participate in our government until attitudes toward women changed much later. (See Chapter 5: Voting. "Are there any grown-ups who aren't allowed to vote?")

★

Why didn't the Founding Fathers make the head of our government a king?

America had fought a bloody war to break away from the tyrannical rule of England's King George III. Americans did not want to start a new nation based on the same system that England had. They felt that the people could rule themselves. So they created a new form of government, one that was run by the people and not by a single person. (See Chapter 2: Our Government.)

★

So is the president the boss of the United States?

Not really. The first words of the Preamble to the Constitution are "We, the people . . . " The people of the United States are the boss of the president, not the other way around. The president, as well as all our representatives, are selected by the people they will lead.

★

But isn't the president of the United States the most powerful person in the world?

You could say that, but in the structure of our government, the president is not as powerful as you might think. Without the cooperation of the public, the Congress, and the courts, he is really powerless.

For instance, the president doesn't determine how the United States spends its money. Every year he has to present a budget to Congress and fight for its approval. And the Congress can pass a bill even if the president vetoes it.

★

A bill? A veto? What does that mean?

A bill is a proposed law. The laws of this country are made by Congress, not by the president. When a bill is approved by the Congress, it is sent to the president. If he signs it, it becomes a law. If he disagrees with the new bill, he can veto, or strike it down. He doesn't sign the bill. Then it goes back to Congress.

If the president vetoes a bill, it can still become a law if two-thirds of the Congress vote in favor of it. The bill will also become law if the president doesn't respond to it within ten days.

The Founding Fathers did not make it easy to pass new laws—on purpose. And they made sure the president's powers were very limited.

★

But isn't the president commander in chief of the armed forces?

Yes, but even there, presidential power is limited. For instance, the president cannot declare war on another country. Only Congress has that power.

★

So what's the point of being commander in chief?

To defend the interests of the United States, the president *does* have the power to order our troops into action without a formal declaration of war. We never officially declared war in the Korean War (1950–1953), the Vietnam War (1957–1975), the Persian Gulf War (1991), or the recent wars in Iraq and Afghanistan. These were "presidential wars."

According to the War Powers Act of 1973, the president has to withdraw our troops after ninety days unless Congress approves continuing the military action.

★

It doesn't sound like the president has much power at all.

The president *does* have enormous influence. The president can recommend new laws be passed, as presidents do in their annual State of the Union address. He is also the leader of a political party. (See Chapter 2: Our Government.) He will help decide that party's positions, support party members in elections, and appoint members of that party to top government jobs.

The president can make treaties with other nations (with the consent of the Senate). He can also grant pardons to people who have been convicted of federal crimes.

And, of course, the president of the United States has the one ultimate power: the decision to use nuclear weapons. When we dropped the atomic bomb to end World War II, President Harry Truman had to make that agonizing decision and take responsibility for it.

That's a lot of power. Plus, the president also has something called "Executive Power."

★

What is "Executive Power"?

It is a special power the president has in times of emergency. When Abraham Lincoln issued the Emancipation Proclamation in 1853 to free the slaves, he didn't get anyone's approval first. The nation was being ripped apart by the Civil War. He felt it was the right thing to do, so he did it.

Similarly, Thomas Jefferson made the decision in 1803 to purchase the Louisiana Territory from France for $15 million. (There are some *houses* today that cost that much money!) The president of the United States doesn't have the power to buy land. But Jefferson saw the opportunity to more than double the size of the country, so he pounced on it before Napoléon, the leader of France, could change his mind. Jefferson didn't get permission from Congress until after the fact.

★

What are the president's responsibilities?

When you watch the news, it may seem like the president's job is to shake hands, attend celebrations, give out awards, get his picture taken, and throw out the first ball at baseball games. Actually, the president of the United States wears many hats and has one of the most difficult jobs in the world.

The official title of the president is "Chief Executive." His duties are many. Take a deep breath. The president must:

Sign bills into law. Prepare an annual budget.

Appoint public officials, generals, ambassadors (with consent of the Senate), and Supreme Court justices (also with consent of the Senate).

He must set foreign policy, maintain relationships with other world leaders, and help them resolve their differences (as President Carter did with Israel and Egypt in 1979). He must oversee military operations, call special sessions of Congress in times of emergency, and keep the Congress informed by giving his annual State of the Union address.

As head of state, the president is the symbol of the United States, so he must do whatever he can to promote American interests.

The first responsibility, when the president is elected, is to make up his cabinet.

★

Can't the president just go to a store and buy a cabinet?

Not *that* cabinet! You see, if you were to sum up the president's job in just two words, it would be to "enforce laws." But obviously, in a nation of more than 300 million people, the president can't do that job alone. The "cabinet" is a group of people who assist the president. They are his experts.

Members of the cabinet include: secretary of state, secretary of the treasury, secretary of defense, attorney general, secretary of the interior, secretary of agriculture, secretary of transportation, and there are also secretaries in charge of veterans affairs, education, energy, housing and urban development, health and human services, labor, and commerce.

Each of these heads of a government department is chosen for his or her knowledge and experience in that particular field. They don't vote; they are advisers. They are selected by the president and must be approved by the Senate.

★

What are the First Lady's responsibilities?

Even though the president's spouse has no stated responsibilities and receives no pay, it is also a very difficult job.

We don't have royalty in the United States, but the wives of our presidents are close to royalty. Their every word, action, and hairstyle are noticed, and criticized. From the beginning, First Ladies have realized they had influence. They each found a way to use that influence, being careful not to appear too powerful, as they are not elected by the people.

"I am in a position where I can do the most good to help the most people," Eleanor Roosevelt said. She traveled the world, held press conferences, gave lectures, spoke on the radio, and wrote newspaper columns fighting for human rights and justice for all Americans. That set the tone for the modern First Lady devoted to social causes.

Lady Bird Johnson campaigned to make the highways of America more beautiful. Betty Ford fought for women's rights and founded a famous center for alcohol and drug rehabilitation. Rosalynn Carter worked for mental health reform. Nancy Reagan led the war on drugs. Barbara Bush and Laura Bush promoted literacy. Hillary Rodham Clinton campaigned to improve the nation's health care system. Michelle Obama fought against childhood obesity.

Someday there will be a female president. If she is married, there will be a "First Gentleman." Like the First Ladies before him, he will carve out his own role.

★

Does the president get paid?

Yes. George Washington, our first president, received a salary of $25,000 a year. That may not seem like much money, but remember that a dollar went a lot farther in 1789. (In fact, it has been said that George Washington threw one across the Delaware River.)

Sorry. A little presidential humor.

In 1873, the presidential salary was doubled, to $50,000. Then it was increased to $75,000 in 1909, to $100,000 in 1949, and to $200,000 in 1969. Today, the president earns $400,000 a year.

The president does not have to pay for his house, his office staff, postage, electricity, or telephone service. He *does* have to pay for his own personal expenses, such as food, parties, and receptions that are not related to government business.

In the late 1920s, baseball star Babe Ruth was earning the then-enormous salary of $80,000. A newspaper reporter asked Ruth if he deserved to be making more money than President Hoover.

"Sure," Ruth replied. "I had a better year than he did."

THE CONSTITUTION (Article II, Section 1):

"The President shall, at stated Times, receive for his Services, a Compensation, which shall neither be encreased nor diminished during the Period for which he shall have been elected, . . . "

★

Where does the president live?

The president lives and works in the White House, in Washington, D.C. The street address is 1600 Pennsylvania Avenue.

The White House was designed by James Hoban in 1792 and was built while George Washington was in office. He was our only president who did not live in the White House.

Over the years the mansion has gone through a lot of changes (the British almost totally burned it down in 1814). Today, the White House has 132 rooms. In addition to the Oval Office, where the president works, and the president's living quarters, the White House has a barber shop, doctor's office, dental clinic, tailor shop, beauty salon, machine shop, plumbing shop, gym, tennis court, basketball court, bowling alley (Nixon once bowled a score of 233), heated pool, game room, and even a movie theater.

The White House is so big, it has thirty-two toilets!

Close to one hundred people work in the White House. Every piece of furniture gets polished daily.

Before 9/11, the White House was open to the public for tours of the first floor. Now, it is necessary to get special permission from your senator or representative to take the tour.

★

Why has there been just one African-American president and not a single female president?

In a word, bigotry. Women were not even allowed to vote until 1920. (See Chapter 5: Voting.) Up until the 1960s, in some parts of our country, African Americans had to attend separate schools, eat in separate restaurants, sleep in separate hotels, use separate bathrooms, and even drink from separate water fountains. Under such conditions, a black or female president of the United States would have been unthinkable.

But that didn't stop their efforts. As far back as 1872, a woman named Victoria Woodhull ran for president representing the Equal Rights Party. Her vice presidential running mate was a black man, freed slave and famous speaker Frederick Douglass.

In more recent years, Shirley Chisholm, who was black and female, made a serious run for the Democratic nomination in 1972. In 1984, Democrat Geraldine Ferraro of New York was the vice presidential running mate of Walter Mondale (they lost the election). Elizabeth Dole ran for the Republican nomination in 1999. Prior to 2008, the most serious attempt by an African American was by the Reverend Jesse Jackson, who attracted a lot of support in 1984 and 1988.

Attitudes toward woman and minority groups have changed dramatically over the last forty years. They now serve as mayors, governors, senators, and representatives all over the country.

Today, most Americans cast their vote for the person they think will do the best job, not the person of a certain gender or skin color. In 2008, African American candidate Barack Obama was elected president. It is only a matter of time until the United States has a female president.

★

Has there ever been a president who wasn't elected to the office?

Yes, once. It was Gerald Ford, the thirty-eighth president.

Here's how it happened: In 1973, Vice President Spiro Agnew was accused of failing to pay his taxes when he was the governor of Maryland. He resigned. Richard Nixon, who was president at the time, appointed Gerald Ford to take Agnew's place as vice president.

As it turned out, the following year President Nixon resigned, and Vice President Ford became the first president who was never elected.

For a more complete story of what happened to President Nixon, see later in this chapter: Has a president ever resigned?

★

What about Lyndon Johnson? Didn't he just get to be president because President Kennedy was assassinated?

Yes, but he had been elected vice president already.

★

How long does the president stay in office?

The king of a country will very often stay in power until he decides to step down, is overthrown, or dies. In the United States, the president holds office for a specific period of time. As it says in the Constitution (Article II, Section I): "He shall hold his Office during the Term of four Years . . . "

When George Washington's first four-year term was over, he ran for reelection and won a second term. Many people wanted Washington to run for a third term, but he refused. After that, it became tradition for the president to serve a maximum of two terms.

In 1940 much of the world was engulfed in war, and America was in the midst of the Great Depression. President Franklin D. Roosevelt was urged to run for a third term of office, and he won. He was our only president to serve more than two terms.

Four years later, with the United States now fighting in World War II, Roosevelt ran for a fourth term, and he won again. He died before that term was over. Roosevelt was president for twelve years.

Many people felt that four terms of office were too many. In 1951, the Twenty-second Amendment to the Constitution was passed, stating, "No person shall be elected to the office of the President more than twice, . . . "

For your information, senators are elected to six-year terms, and members of the House of Representatives are elected to two-year terms.

★

Why is the president's term of office four years?

When the Founding Fathers wrote the Constitution, they argued quite a bit about how long the president's term of office should be. First, they decided on six years. Then they changed their mind and decided it should be eleven. Then it was fifteen. Then it was seven. Finally, they agreed on four years.

Four years gives the president enough time to get used to the job and get good work accomplished. It is not so long that a poor president can do much damage to the nation.

Abraham Lincoln once said, "no administration, by any extreme of wickedness or folly, can very seriously injure the government in the short space of four years."

★

Does the president always run for a second term of office?

No. James Polk, Rutherford Hayes, and Lyndon Johnson chose not to run for a second term.

Johnson became president when John F. Kennedy was assassinated in 1963. He ran for reelection the following year and won. But Johnson received so much criticism for the way he was handling the war in Vietnam that he announced in March of 1968 that he would not pursue another term of office.

Not every president has enjoyed being president. When his term of office was over and he was leaving the White House, President Taft said, "I am glad to be going. This is the lonesomest place in the world."

★

Has anyone ever been president two separate times?

Yes. Grover Cleveland was both the twenty-second president and the twenty-fourth president. A Democrat, he won the 1884 election, but he lost when he ran for reelection in 1888.

As he and his wife were moving out of the White House, Mrs. Cleveland told the staff to keep everything just the way it was because she expected to move back four years later. As it turned out, she was right. Grover Cleveland was nominated by the Democrats again in 1892, and won.

★

What is a "lame duck" president?

A president who is coming to the end of his second term of office is called a "lame duck." He can't run for reelection. He can't get much accomplished, because he won't be around very long as the nation's leader. In other words, he is not a very effective president.

Some say the term "lame duck" was originally British. Others say it comes from hunting. A wounded duck, after all, does not make a very good trophy. And it certainly does not make a very good duck, either.

★

What does the president do after his term is over?

Many of our presidents have retired to a life of leisure (Washington, Madison, Monroe, Eisenhower, to name a few) or to write their autobiography. Others remained very active.

Thomas Jefferson helped start the University of Virginia. Herbert Hoover became the head of the Famine Emergency Commission. Benjamin Harrison practiced law. William Taft was appointed chief justice of the Supreme Court.

Ulysses Grant toured the world. Theodore Roosevelt went to South America to explore a river. Jimmy Carter helped rival nations resolve their differences, and helped renovate homes for the poor with the organization Habitat For Humanity.

Two of our presidents ran for office after their presidency was over. Andrew Johnson was elected senator from Tennessee. John Quincy Adams was elected to Congress by the voters of Massachusetts. Some people felt it was a disgrace that the former president of the United States would "lower himself" to becoming a congressman. But Adams proudly stated that no man is disgraced by serving his country. He spent seventeen years in Congress, and helped establish the Smithsonian Institution.

★

How many presidents have we had?

President Barack Obama was the forty-fourth president of the United States. Turn to the back of this book if you'd like to see a complete list of United States presidents and their political party, term of office, and the date and place of their birth and death.

★

Why do people always seem to criticize the president?

We have all different kinds of people in this country. Rich and poor. Old and young. People of different ancestry. People of different racial groups, religions, and political parties. Many of those groups have differing opinions, interests, and desires.

In some other countries, citizens are not allowed to express these opinions. In 1989, a large group of young people gathered in China to criticize the way the government was run. Government soldiers arrested them, imprisoned them and, in some cases, shot them.

In America, we have freedom of speech: the freedom to express ourselves and our beliefs. We can think and say what we want about the government, even if the government doesn't like it. It is perhaps the most important right granted in the Bill of Rights.

As a result, when people and groups disagree with the president, they are going to let him know. They hold protest marches. They write angry letters to newspapers. They complain about him on talk shows. They publish books criticizing him, and create posters, cartoons, and Web sites ridiculing him. Sometimes people just don't like the president, period.

When bad things happen in the country, like when the economy is not doing well, it is the president who usually gets the blame. And let's face it: Presidents are only human, and sometimes they make mistakes. When that happens, the president may even be criticized by people who support him.

Abraham Lincoln once said, "If I were to try to read, much less answer, all the attacks made on me, this shop might as well be closed for any other business."

In nearly all cases, criticism of the president is a healthy expression of our freedom of speech. But in a few cases, opponents of the president have gone beyond their freedom of speech and actually tried to harm him.

★

How is the president protected from harm?

Our early presidents would walk the streets unprotected. It wasn't until 1864 that bodyguards were assigned to protect the president. Ironically, President Lincoln was assassinated a year later. But it wasn't until President McKinley was assassinated in 1901 that Secret Service agents accompanied the president wherever he went.

These days, security around the president (and his family) is very tight. An eight-foot iron fence with crash-proof gates surrounds the White House. Concrete barriers outside are there to stop a truck. Pressure sensors on the lawn can send a signal to launch ground-to-air missiles that can take out a tank. There is a bomb shelter in the basement under the East Wing.

White House guests must pass through a metal detector. Dogs sniff for explosives. When the president sits down to eat, a food taster has checked to make sure the meal has not been poisoned. When he gives a speech, he stands behind a bulletproof podium.

One reason why the White House has a pool, tennis court, and other facilities is because it is very dangerous for the president to go out in public. When he does, he travels in a bullet-proof railroad car and bullet-proof limousine. Weeks in advance of a presidential appearance, the location is carefully scouted to make sure it is safe. The president is always accompanied by about a dozen armed Secret Service agents. Sometimes he is even wearing bullet-proof clothing.

All this security may seem unnecessary, but four of our presidents have been assassinated (Lincoln, Garfield, McKinley, and Kennedy). Attempts have been made on the lives of three others (Truman, Ford, and Reagan). Candidates for the presidency have survived assassination attempts (George Wallace and Theodore Roosevelt), and in 1968 Robert Kennedy was killed while campaigning for president.

The Secret Service has files on hundreds of individuals who have made threats against the president. This is why security for the president and presidential candidates must be taken very seriously.

★

What happens if the president dies while in office?

The Constitution states it very clearly (Article II, Section I): "In case of the Removal of the President from Office or of his Death or Resignation, the Vice President shall become President."

William Henry Harrison became president on March 4, 1841. It was a rainy day when Harrison took his oath of office. He gave an inaugural speech that lasted an hour and forty-five minutes. He caught a cold, and it turned into pneumonia. Exactly one month after he became president, Harrison died. His was the shortest presidency in American history. Vice President John Tyler became president.

Eight of our presidents have died while in office (William Harrison, Zachary Taylor, Abraham Lincoln, James Garfield, William McKinley, Warren Harding,

Franklin D. Roosevelt, and John F. Kennedy). In each case, the vice president became president, and there was a smooth transition of power.

★

What if the president and the vice president die?

That, fortunately, has never happened. But if it ever does, the rules of "succession" are in place. If something were to happen to the vice president, the Speaker of the House would become president (the Speaker presides over the House of Representatives and is chosen by them).

If the Speaker of the House dies, the president pro tempore ("for the time being") becomes president. The president pro tempore is the senator who presides over the Senate when the vice president is not available.

And if something were to happen to the president pro tempore, members of the cabinet would take over, starting with the secretary of state, the secretary of the treasury, the secretary of defense, and the attorney general.

★

What if the president doesn't die, but is unconscious?

When President Garfield was shot in 1881, he hovered between life and death for a long time before passing away. This brought up this sticky question: What would happen if the president couldn't do his job and the vice president took over . . . and then the president recovered?

It was not until 1967 that this problem was solved. According to the Twenty-fifth Amendment to the Constitution, the vice president and the cabinet will decide if the vice president should take over the duties of the president. If the president recovers, he resumes his duties by declaring in writing that he is able. If the vice president and cabinet disagree with the president, Congress can vote (by a two-thirds majority) to prevent the president from returning to his job.

★

Has a president ever resigned?

Once. Richard Nixon, the thirty-seventh president. Here's what happened.

On the evening of June 17, 1972, five men were arrested for breaking in and burglarizing the headquarters of the Democratic National Committee at the Watergate complex in Washington, D.C. They had planted telephone bugs and taken photos. It was discovered that these men were hired by the Committee to Reelect the President.

Several of the president's top aides were put on trial and convicted of this criminal act. President Nixon claimed he had nothing to do with the break-in. But secret tape recordings the president made himself revealed that Nixon *was* involved in trying to cover up the crime.

The president was charged with obstruction of justice, abuse of presidential power, and refusal to obey congressional subpoenas. Congress began the process of removing him from office. Two days after the president was informed there were enough votes to impeach him, he resigned on August 9, 1974.

★

What does "impeach" mean?

Some people think the word "impeach" means "to throw out of office." It doesn't. To impeach someone is to officially accuse them of serious wrongdoing in the performance of their duties.

The Founding Fathers wanted to make sure there was a way to remove a president who had done damage to the country. They created a process called impeachment. So far, no president has been kicked out of office. But two have been impeached.

In 1868, President Andrew Johnson had angered many members of Congress. He wanted to continue President Lincoln's policy of rebuilding the South after the Civil War. "The Radical Republicans" wanted to punish the Southern states and place them under military rule. They moved to impeach Johnson.

The House of Representatives has the power to charge the president with committing a crime. They voted 126-47 to impeach President Johnson.

The Senate has the responsibility to put the president on trial if he is impeached. If two-thirds of the Senate vote to convict, the president is removed from office. In President Johnson's case, the Senate fell one vote short of conviction, so the president remained in office.

More recently, President Clinton was impeached during his second term. He, too, was acquitted by the Senate.

> THE CONSTITUTION (Article II, Section IV):
> "The President, Vice-President and all civil Officers
> of the United States, shall be removed from Office
> on Impeachment for, and Conviction of, Treason,
> Bribery, or other high Crimes and Misdemeanors."

★

Why does the president get a twenty-one-gun salute?

The number twenty-one represents the year 1776, when America declared its independence. Add it up: one plus seven plus seven plus six equals twenty-one.

★

CHAPTER 2

★ ★ ★ ★ ★ ★ ★ ★ ★ ★ ★ ★ ★ ★ ★ ★ ★ ★

Our Government

What system of government do we have in America?

Our system of government is called a presidential-legislative democracy. In other words, power is shared by a president and a lawmaking body.

"Democracy" comes from the Greek words "demos," which means "the community," and "kratos," which means "sovereign power." In other words, a democracy is government by the community, or by the people. A democratic government is one in which the people vote to elect other people (representatives) to make important decisions and run the nation.

Abraham Lincoln probably summed up democracy most simply in his 1863 Gettysburg Address, when he said we had a "government of the people, by the people, for the people."

When our country was founded in the 1700s, democracy was a revolutionary idea. Most nations were led by kings in those days. They had become kings simply because their fathers had been kings, and they ruled for life. To you, democracy may seem to be such an obvious way to run a government, but back then it was really a big experiment.

★

Why was democracy chosen as our system of government?

When the Founding Fathers gathered in Philadelphia in 1787, they didn't know in advance what kind of government they were going to create. They *did* know that the tyrannical British government under King George III was not the way to go. They had many different opinions. They argued a lot among themselves. Gradually, over a period of several months, they developed a new system of government. They put it in writing in a document called the Constitution.

★

What is the Constitution?

The Constitution, in just 4,550 words, outlines the basic ideas of the United States government: liberty, equality, and justice. These are simple ideas, of course. But millions of people have come from all over the world because the countries they lived in did not have this kind of government.

You can see the original document of the Constitution today in the National Archives in Washington, D.C.

★

Wait a minute. Liberty? Equality? Didn't they have slavery in America back then?

Yes. The concepts of liberty and equality have changed dramatically since 1787. The Founding Fathers did not abolish slavery in the Declaration of Independence when they wrote, ". . . all men are created equal . . ." In fact, the author of those words, Thomas Jefferson, was a slave owner. Jefferson and his colleagues did not consider African Americans equal to European Americans. They did not consider women to be equal to men.

But they *did* realize that ideas change over time. Because of this, they made it so the Constitution could be amended, or changed.

The Bill of Rights (1791) included the first ten amendments to the Constitution, guaranteeing American citizens basic freedoms (speech, press, religion, and so on). The Thirteenth Amendment abolished slavery, and the Nineteenth Amendment gave women the right to vote. So far there have been twenty-seven amendments to the Constitution.

★

Was the United States the first democracy?

No. In the 5th and 6th centuries B.C., Greek city-states held elections to choose their leaders. The ancient Romans also had a form of democracy. But until the 1700s, almost all governments were headed by kings and queens. The United States was the first country that was founded from the start as a democracy.

Today, many countries around the world are democracies.

★

What other systems of government are there?

There are many different forms of government. Here are a few.

Anarchy: No government. The people rule themselves. An anarchist would believe that government is unnecessary and harmful.

Aristocracy: Government by an elite few who were born into families of wealth and power.

Monarchy: Government headed by one king, queen, or emperor. If that person has unlimited power, it's called an absolute monarchy. If the monarch's power is limited by a constitution, it's called a constitutional monarchy.

One party: One political party has all the power.

Dominant party: One party rules, but others are allowed to exist.

Despotism: Government by a single person (despot) who has absolute, unlimited power. That person would also be called a "dictator."

People generally think of communism and socialism as forms of government, but in fact they are really economic systems. In communism, all property is owned in common and the nation's economy is run by the government, not by the people. Socialism aims to eliminate the idea of rich people and poor people by having the government control the production and distribution of goods.

★

How does democracy work in America?

One of the biggest concerns of the Founding Fathers was that one person or a group of people might gain power, take over the country, and make decisions that would not be in the interests of the people. For this reason, they very carefully worked out a federal government with three branches.

1. Legislative: This is the Congress. Its main job is to make laws. There are two "houses" of Congress: the Senate and the House of Representatives. There are a hundred senators (two from each state). The number of Representatives depends on the population of each state.

2. Executive. The president, whose job is to enforce laws.

3. Judicial. The Supreme Court, whose job is to interpret laws and decide if they are constitutional.

This "separation of powers" was designed to force the three branches of government to make compromises and work together for the good of all. You may have heard the term "checks and balances." One branch of the government checks, or controls, the power of the other branches. In doing so, no single branch is allowed to become too powerful.

★

Do checks and balances work?

Usually, yes. Democracy works slowly. With our system, it sometimes takes a long time to get things done.

This was done on purpose to prevent hasty, short-sighted decisions.

For example, if a king wakes up one morning and decides that all people with blond hair should be put in jail, the next day the police will start rounding up blondes.

But if the president of the United States woke up one morning with the same idea, he would have to suggest that Congress pass a law imprisoning all blondes. Congress would discuss it and argue over it for a long time. If they voted to put that law into effect, the Supreme Court could rule that it was unconstitutional (in conflict with the Constitution).

A dumb idea like that is unlikely to become law in America. With our system of checks and balances, there is time for all opinions to be heard, arguments to be made, people to change their minds.

There was only one time in American history when our system of government did not work as planned. It was in the 1850s, when the people in the Southern states favored slavery and people in the Northern states wanted it abolished. Both sides had very firmly held beliefs. Neither side was willing to compromise on the issue.

As a result, the Southern states broke away to form their own country. The Civil War had to be fought to bring the United States together again.

★

Where do Democrats and Republicans fit into our system of government?

The Democrats and Republicans are two "political parties." That is, they are groups of people organized to direct the policies of the government.

When our country began, the Founding Fathers did not want political parties. They wanted to create "united states" and they felt opposing parties would divide people. When George Washington was elected the first president, he was not a member of any political party.

But people don't always agree about everything. A farmer in Georgia has very different concerns and opinions than that of a Massachusetts shop owner. Your parents may have very different concerns and opinions than that of the people who live across the street.

Even while George Washington was president, political parties were formed by people who had differing ideas about the way our government should be run. Alexander Hamilton and his followers believed in a very strong central government. They called themselves the Federalists. Thomas Jefferson and his followers believed in more power for the states. They called themselves the Democratic Republicans.

Later, other political parties were formed. The Whigs wanted Congress to be the strongest branch of the government. They got William Henry Harrison elected president in 1840, and Zachary Taylor elected in 1848.

The American Party was formed in the 1850s to fight the surge of immigrants coming into the United States. (They were called the "Know-Nothing Party" because when they were asked what they stood for, they would reply, "I know nothing.")

None of those political parties exists anymore. Today there are two main political parties in America: the Republican Party and the Democratic Party. That's why we call it "a two-party system." The symbol for the Republicans is the elephant, and the symbol for the Democrats is a donkey.

★

What do the Republicans and Democrats stand for?

There are many different issues that concern Americans. On some issues, the two main political parties agree or come fairly close to agreement. On other issues, they oppose one another. Opinions are constantly shifting, and there is a wide range of different opinions even within the same party.

But in very general terms, the main difference between the two parties is this: The Democrats believe in a strong federal government, with the government playing an active role in people's lives by the use of federal programs. The Republicans believe in less government interference in people's lives, especially when it comes to economic issues.

★

What about people whose opinion is somewhere in the middle?

That would be almost everybody. People's opinions are not always black/white, yes/no, good/bad. All people who call themselves Democrats don't necessarily share the same opinion, and neither do all Republicans.

One individual may feel very strongly in favor of one idea. A second person may totally oppose that idea. And a third person may feel both sides are partly correct.

You may hear the terms "left," "right," and "center" when people talk about politics. People who are "on the left" are sometimes referred to as "liberals." People who are "on the right" are sometimes referred to as "conservatives."

In general, liberals believe in a strong central government, and in using the power of the government to help people solve problems, even at the expense of businesses and wealthy people. Liberals are usually Democrats.

In general, conservatives believe in a small government that puts fewer restrictions on people or businesses, and individuals are expected to solve their own problems. Conservatives are usually Republicans.

Some people have opinions that are extremely "left wing" or extremely "right wing." They are often referred to as "extremists." People who don't hold such extreme views are called "moderates." You may hear about a candidate who has moved "to the left" on an issue or "toward the center." Some people may be called "middle-of-the-roaders."

All of these people may be patriotic Americans who love their country, but they have different opinions about the way the government should be run.

★

Which political party is the best?

There's no "best." Choosing which political party to support is a personal decision. As you grow up, you will examine all the issues that affect Americans and you will decide for yourself which party or candidates have opinions that match your own. The reason why kids are not allowed to vote is because they haven't had the chance to think about these issues and make informed decisions about them.

★

Which party has won the most elections?

Between 1778 and 1996, Americans elected nineteen Democrats to the presidency, seventeen Republicans,

four Whigs, and two Federalists. The Democrats domi-
nated before 1860. Starting with Abraham Lincoln (the
first Republican president), the Republicans domi-
nated from 1860 to 1928. They won the presidency thirteen times while the Democrats only won four times.
Starting in 1932, the Democrats caught up, winning
nine times while the Republicans won seven times.

The nation's mood seems to swing back and forth.
We might choose Republicans for a few elections, then
we tire of their candidates and vote Democrats into
office. That's just the way politics goes.

★

**Are American citizens forced to join a political
party?**

No. You've heard the expression "It's a free country."
Nobody can tell a voter who to vote for or what party
to join (if any).

When you turn eighteen years old and register to
vote, you will be given a card to fill out. There will be a
space on that card that says "political party." You can
write "Republican" or you can write "Democrat." If you
are not sure or simply don't feel comfortable with the

positions of either party, you can write "Independent." (See Chapter 5: Voting.)

You may also decide, for reasons of privacy, that you want to keep your choice personal. In that case, you may write "decline to state."

Whatever you write on that card, you can still vote in the presidential election for whichever candidate you prefer. Registered Republicans can vote for a Democratic candidate, and registered Democrats can vote for a Republican candidate. Or, if they want to, voters can choose a third-party candidate.

★

What is a third party?

The Republicans and Democrats are not the only political parties in America. They are just the *major* parties. There is also the Libertarian Party, the Socialist Workers Party, the American Independent Party, the Citizens Party and several others. A man named Gus Hall ran for the American presidency in 1972, 1980, and 1984 as head of the Communist Party.

There have been many attempts to launch a third political party in America, some more successful than others. Often, third-party candidates have run because of one issue they considered important that the Democrats and Republicans were not addressing. Third-party candidates have served to introduce different ideas and forced the Democrats and Republicans to pay attention to issues they would have otherwise ignored.

★

Has a third-party candidate ever won the presidency?

No. But they have influenced presidential elections. In 1912, a group of Republicans split off to form the Progressive Party. They nominated former president Theodore Roosevelt as their candidate for president.

As it turned out, Roosevelt got more votes than the Republican candidate (William H. Taft). But the Democratic candidate, Woodrow Wilson, got more votes than either of them, and he won the election.

If Roosevelt's votes and Taft's votes had been combined into one candidate, that candidate would have beaten Wilson. The Progressive Party had "split" the Republican vote, which gave the election to the Democrats. Whenever there is a third party, the two major parties are very concerned that votes will be "drained" away from them and will prevent them from winning a majority.

Although no third-party candidate has won a presidential election, several have put on impressive showings. In 1968, George Wallace and the American Independent Party attracted nearly 10 million votes (out of 73 million). In 1992, Ross Perot and the Reform Party got 19 million votes.

★

CHAPTER 3

★ ★ ★ ★ ★ ★ ★ ★ ★ ★ ★ ★ ★ ★ ★

The Campaign

What is a campaign?

If you look in Webster's Student Dictionary, the word "campaign" is defined as "a series of battles or other military actions having a special goal." It could certainly be said that the campaign for president is sometimes like a war.

The campaign is everything that leads up to the election. That would include all the advertisements you see on TV, radio, billboards, and in the newspaper. It also includes the bumper stickers, buttons, and signs you see on people's lawns. It means rallies, fund-raisers, debates, town meetings, press conferences, photo opportunities, and speeches. When you see candidates marching in parades, shaking hands, and kissing babies, they are campaigning.

In the weeks and months leading up to the election, the candidates will travel around the country, meet as many voters as possible, explain their positions on all kinds of issues, and try to show voters that they would make a better president than their opponent.

The candidates will work very hard to convince voters to support them. Working with a campaign manager, they will plan the strategy of the campaign very carefully. The strategy they use may be the difference between winning and losing the election.

★

What sorts of strategies do they use?

An election campaign, like a battlefield campaign, is usually planned to the smallest detail. Everything the candidate does is aimed at attracting votes. Careful attention is paid to what the candidates say, what they do, what they wear, how they present themselves, where they go, who they are seen shaking hands with, what books they read, and even how much money they spend on a haircut. Every day the candidates try to make headlines, or get on the evening news.

If the candidate was a war hero (like Dwight Eisenhower), movie star (Ronald Reagan), or athlete (Bill Bradley), they will do everything they can to take advantage of their popularity. If they have a weakness (and everybody does), they will try to hide it. And if their opponent has a weakness, they will attack it.

★

That doesn't sound very nice.

Politics can get ugly at times. We are all bombarded with images of the candidates in an election year. Sometimes we see them saying positive things about what they plan to do for the country. Other times we see them (or people speaking on behalf of them) saying negative things about their opponent.

Candidates routinely are accused of scandalous behavior, having no experience, being dumb, favoring the rich, dodging the draft, being a warmonger, or not having the courage to fight.

When a candidate has a rally or speech, his staff may print up signs and give them out to people so the crowd will look enthusiastic on TV. They will "plant" questions that will give the candidate the chance to give an answer that makes him look good. They may even plant people at an *opponent's* rally to ask embarrassing questions.

There have been cases of TV lines being cut and other "dirty tricks" being pulled to win an election. In Chapter 1, you read about the Watergate burglars breaking into an office to get information that would help the president get elected. Things like this do happen.

★

How do citizens know what to believe?

Voters have to pay attention and stay informed. They should read newspapers and newsmagazines. They should find out how the candidates stand on each issue. They should be looking at what each candidate has done in other elective offices they held.

These days, a lot of the presidential campaign is conducted through television. Question everything you see in a candidate's TV commercials. Always remember that the candidate is trying to show himself off in the best possible way. You cannot make a fair evaluation just by watching TV commercials.

★

How did candidates campaign before TV?

It may sound hard to believe, but in America's early days it was considered undignified for a candidate to go out and solicit votes. You didn't see George Washington kissing babies and stopping into neighborhoods to sample ethnic foods. (Things might have been different if there had been TV, or even still photography, back then!)

In 1828, Andrew Jackson changed all that. He went out and gave speeches to small groups of people, asking for their support. These came to be called "stump" speeches because the candidate would use a tree stump as a makeshift stage. Jackson defeated President John Quincy Adams, and candidates have campaigned for votes ever since.

The supporters of William Henry Harrison used brass bands, bonfires, and torchlight parades to get people excited about their candidate. It worked. Harrison beat President Martin Van Buren in 1840.

By 1869, railroads had stretched from the Atlantic Ocean to the Pacific. For the first time, candidates could travel far and wide looking for votes. The "whistle-stop" tour began. At each stop, the candidate would go to the back of the train and make a short speech to the people who gathered there. When the train whistle blew, the speech was over, and it was off to the next town. William Jennings Bryant logged 18,000 miles and countless speeches in his 1896 campaign.

(The whistle-stop tour was pretty much over by 1952, when both candidates used airplanes to fly around the country.)

By 1924, radio became an important campaign tool. Candidates would still travel, but for the first time they could send their words all over the country without having to *go* all over the country.

Starting in the 1950s, TV became the most important campaigning tool.

Candidates suddenly had to pay close attention to the way they dressed and the way they looked on camera.

Candidates have always used the technology of their time to campaign for president. Nowadays, all the candidates and political parties have a Web site.

(See the back of this book for some Web addresses you might want to check out.) With the Internet, the candidate doesn't have to go to the voter; the voter can go to the candidate.

Even in the information age, candidates still want to travel around the nation and meet face-to-face with voters. These days, many candidates tour the country by bus.

A candidate's campaign strategy will change week to week, sometimes day to day. Candidates watch polls very carefully to see if their strategies are working.

★

Isn't watching a pole a big waste of time?

Not pole, *poll.* A poll is a sort of fake election. During the election campaign, surveys are constantly being taken to see how voters feel about the candidates. Long before Election Day, you will hear that Candidate X is ahead in the polls, or Candidate Y is catching up in the polls. These polls are usually taken by calling hundreds of voters on the phone and asking them a series of questions. Polls are conducted very carefully, very scientifically.

★

What difference does it make what voters say before Election Day?

Candidates often plan their strategy according to the polls. If the polls say a candidate is weak in a state, he may devote more time campaigning there. If the polls say he is so far behind that he can't win in that state, he may decide it would be smarter to spend his time and money elsewhere. And if the polls say he's *certain* to win that state, he will probably decide not to spend his time and money campaigning there, either. Some candidates will drop out of the race entirely if the polls suggest it is a hopeless cause.

The polls are also watched carefully to see how voters are responding to a candidate's views. If the polls show that the candidate's position on a certain issue is unpopular, he may change his position. Politicians are often accused of following the polls rather than expressing their true beliefs.

Voters also pay attention to the polls. If the polls say a candidate is way behind, people may feel they don't want to "waste" their vote in a losing cause, even if they agree with that candidate's views. They might decide to cast their vote for somebody who has a better chance of winning. And if the polls are predicting that one candidate has an overwhelming lead just before Election Day, a lot of people won't even bother voting. They figure their vote isn't needed.

★

Do voters have to tell a poll-taker how they're going to vote?

Absolutely not. Many people feel that poll-taking is an invasion of their privacy. We have a "secret ballot" in this country and nobody has to tell anyone else who they intend to vote for.

Polls are often criticized for being inaccurate. People who happen to be home a lot (the elderly, parents with babies, the unemployed) often respond, but others do not. Plus, as many as eight out of ten people simply refuse to be interviewed for polls. (Did they take a poll to come up with that statistic?)

On the other hand, some people want to tell the *world* they are giving their endorsement to a particular candidate.

★

What's an endorsement?

Have you noticed how celebrities appear in ads, billboards, and commercials, saying they wear a particular brand of sneaker or eat a particular kind of breakfast cereal? When they do this, they are giving their *endorsement* to that product, and they are generally paid a lot of money to do it.

Presidential candidates want endorsements, too. If a movie star, athlete, or other celebrity comes out in support of Candidate X, fans of that celebrity may decide to vote for Candidate X, too. Candidates will also seek the endorsement of local politicians or influential groups like the United Auto Workers or the Teamsters Union.

Most newspapers will endorse a candidate for president, and thousands of readers will vote for that candidate as a result. When you read your newspaper in an election year, pay close attention to see how it reports on each candidate. In some papers, you may detect a bias in favor of the candidate the paper is endorsing. There may be more articles written about a preferred candidate, or longer articles, and more flattering ones.

★

When does the campaign for president begin?

Sometimes it is said that a presidential campaign begins the day after the last Election Day. In fact, it can begin even earlier than that. Some candidates spend their whole careers working to reach the presidency.

But generally, the campaign for president begins about one year before Election Day in November. The presidential primaries begin in January, and things really heat up in the nine or ten weeks between Labor Day and Election Day (November 6 in 2012).

★

What are primaries?

Primaries are local elections that are held months before the national election. They serve to narrow down the list of possible candidates.

You see, there may be many Democrats who want to be the Democratic nominee for president. There may be many Republicans who want to be the Republican nominee. All these people can't represent their political party. Each party has to choose *one* person who they believe has the best chance of winning the presidential election in November. So a series of primary elections are held in many states to determine who that person will be.

Primaries have only been around since the 1970s. Before that, each party's candidate was chosen by party officials (in "smoke-filled rooms," it was said, because so many people smoked cigarettes and cigars back then). Regular people couldn't vote on it.

In the 2012 election, the state of New Hampshire held the first primary, on January 10. It was followed by South Carolina and Florida. Seven states held primaries on March 6 ("Super Tuesday"). The last primary, in Utah, took place on June 26.

By the middle of the primary season, it is usually pretty clear who the party's nominee for president is going to be. Candidates who did poorly in the primaries or ran out of money will probably have dropped out of the race by then and thrown their support behind the "front-runner" or leader, who has accumulated the most delegates.

★

ELECTION!

Huh? What's a delegate?

This is where things might get confusing. When people vote in the primary elections, they are not voting directly for their favorite candidate. Instead, they are voting for delegates, or representatives. These delegates may be mayors, state legislators, county commissioners, or other local politicians. Each state has a certain number of delegates, depending upon its population. And each delegate is pledged to cast a vote for a certain candidate at the party's national convention.

★

What is a national convention?

In the summer leading up to Election Day, the Democrats and Republicans each gather in a major American city and hold what appears to be a four-day party for themselves. It takes place in a huge auditorium. There are balloons, banners, horns, confetti, and songs. Thousands of reporters cover the festivities. The whole thing is broadcast on TV, and it is called the national convention.

This is where the party officially selects its nominee for president.

Before the 1970s, nobody knew who the nominee was going to be before the national convention. But because of the primary elections that have already taken place in individual states, it is usually obvious who the winner is. The convention serves mainly to get the nation excited about the party and the candidate.

Thousands of delegates from all over the country attend the convention. For the first few days they hear speeches by important party leaders (who may very well be running for president in the next election). Then the states vote (in alphabetical order) to choose the party's candidate for president.

Each delegate has one vote and, to repeat, the delegates are already pledged to the candidate who won the primary election. The representative for Alabama might stand up and announce, "The great state of Alabama casts its votes for . . . John Doe!"

When all the states have voted, the candidate who won the majority of votes is announced as the party's nominee for president.

Finally, on the last night of the convention, that

candidate will stand before the party and make an acceptance speech. Members of the party who voted for other candidates will attempt to put aside their differences and work together to win the election in November.

That doesn't always happen. In 1948, a group of Democrats from southern states walked out of the national convention because they disagreed with Harry Truman's position on civil rights. (He won, anyway.)

Besides choosing a candidate for president, the first order of business at the convention is creating the party's platform.

★

Platform? Can't they just stand on the stage?

Not *that* kind of platform. A platform is a statement of a political party's policies. Each party wants to state its position on important issues Americans care about: defense spending, health care, the environment, taxes, education, gun control, abortion, foreign policy, and so on. Each one of these issues makes up a "plank" in the platform. The platform is discussed and approved at the national convention, before the vote is taken to choose the nominee for president. Voters should look at each party's platform and decide which one shares their views.

★

What is a debate?

A debate is a discussion in which two (or sometimes more) candidates meet face-to-face. For many voters, the first debate between the Democratic and Republican candidates is the highlight of the presidential campaign. Finally, we get a chance to see the candidates slug it out, live, under pressure, with no prepared scripts or advisers.

In reality, presidential debates have been a lot like the Super Bowl—a lot of hype, but a pretty uninteresting contest. This tends to happen because both candidates are very skillful and practiced speechmakers. With hundreds of millions of voters from every part of the country watching, the candidates are extremely careful not to make a mistake or say anything that might offend a large group of people. As a result, they usually play it safe, and there is no obvious winner or loser.

The most famous presidential debates took place between John F. Kennedy and Richard Nixon in 1960. They had four debates, and it was the first time the entire nation watched the candidates go at it on television.

What made these debates so famous was that Kennedy, a little-known senator at the time, held his own against then-Vice President Nixon. Kennedy became a national figure as a result of the debates; many people believe the debates won him the election.

Abraham Lincoln and Stephen A. Douglas had seven very famous debates in 1858. But they were running for the Illinois Senate, not the presidency.

There is no rule that there have to be presidential debates. There were none in 1964, 1968, or 1972. But these days the public expects the candidates for the two major parties to debate on live TV.

When you watch the presidential debates on TV, pay careful attention to what the candidates say. Do they answer the questions asked of them? Or do they give a confusing response that indicates they prefer to avoid the question? Sometimes they will change the subject entirely, and their answer has nothing to do with the question.

It is up to the voters to determine if a candidate would make a good president, or is simply a good debater.

★

How much money does it cost to run for president?

A *lot*. There's no exact figure, and it's going up all the time. Millions. Many millions! Some sources will say fifty million or more. By the time you are able to vote, the number may be over a billion dollars.

★

Wow! Why does running for president cost so much money?

The candidate has to pay for all the planes, trains, helicopters, and limousines that will take him and his staff around the country. He has to hire speechwriters, consultants, advisers, researchers, a press secretary, a campaign manager, and an advertising agency.

Office space has to be rented, and campaign head-quarters in all fifty states have to be staffed, heated, and air-conditioned. Telephone bills and mailing costs are enormous. Then there are buttons, T-shirts, posters, and so on.

But the biggest expense is from all those radio and television commercials you are bombarded with in an election year. Thirty seconds of airtime in the middle of a popular TV show can cost hundreds of thousands of dollars.

If you can reach millions of people through TV, why don't candidates just campaign by TV?

TV *does* reach almost everybody, but candidates don't always want to give the same message to everybody. If you want to get votes of farmers, you want to talk about what you will do to help farmers and their families. If you want to reach elderly people or people in a specific ethnic group, you want to give them a very different message from the one you gave to farmers. Going out on the road enables candidates to target their message better than they can on television.

Also, people running for office want to go out among the voters so they can see how the voters are responding to their message. They want to feel the voters' enthusiasm. Voters, too, want to see the candidates in person. On TV, the message only goes one way.

★

If a presidential campaign costs so much money, doesn't that mean you have to be wealthy to run?

No (but it helps!). To make a serious run for the presidency requires that a candidate spend a year or two doing nothing but campaigning for president. Few working people can afford to do that. But candidates do not ordinarily pay for their campaign out of their own pocket. Instead, they accept contributions.

★

Couldn't a wealthy person just give millions of dollars to get somebody elected and then tell them how to run the country?

Yes. People have found all sorts of ingenious and perfectly legal ways to elect candidates who share their views and will act in their interest. Politicians are constantly arguing over how to make the process fair to all candidates. All the candidates should have the opportunity to get their message out, and voters should be able to make contributions to the candidate of their choice.

Most people agree that it costs far too much money to run for president, which means that politicians have to spend far too much of their time raising money. And once they get elected, they are indebted to those who donated money to help them win the election.

★

Why doesn't the government just put a limit on how much a candidate can spend?

An effort was made to do just that. But in 1976 the Supreme Court ruled that putting a limit on campaign spending was a violation of free speech. And in 2010, the Supreme Court ruled in the Citizens United case that corporations and unions could spend unlimited amounts of money on political campaigns.

★

Why don't they just ban TV ads entirely? Wouldn't that make it fair?

No. Very well-known national figures would be perfectly happy if there were no TV ads. The public is already familiar with them. But what about a little-known governor or congressperson? These candidates want TV ads so they can become more well-known.

★

Why doesn't the government just pay for the campaign?

It does, partly. When your parents fill out their income tax form each year, they can check off a yes/no box that says: "Presidential Election Campaign. Do you want $3 to go to this fund?"

The government takes that money to generate what are called "matching funds." That means for every dollar the candidate raises, the government will give that candidate a dollar to finance the campaign. So if a million dollars is raised, the candidate gets another million dollars from the government.

To qualify for these matching funds, the candidate

has to accept certain rules and limitations about how they can raise money. If the candidate chooses not to accept matching funds, he can spend as much money as he can raise.

★

Can candidates just use their own money if they want to?

Sure. Especially in recent elections, a few wealthy people have chosen to run for president and finance their campaign with their own money.

Publisher Steve Forbes has run for president twice, spending $53 million of his own money. Ross Perot spent millions of dollars in 1992 to run half-hour television commercials explaining his opinions. In 1999 and 2012, real estate mogul Donald Trump seriously considered making a run for the presidency. So far, none of these candidates has won the presidency.

★

CHAPTER 4

★ ★ ★ ★ ★ ★ ★ ★ ★ ★ ★ ★ ★ ★ ★ ★

Candidates

Can anyone run for president?

Yes, but not anyone can *be* president. There are three simple requirements for a person to be president of the United States.

First, you have to be at least thirty-five years old, which lets out all the readers of this book. The Founding Fathers believed that a person should have many years of experience in government before that person was ready to lead the nation. They were probably right.

Second, you have to be born in the United States. If your parents took a trip overseas and you were born in England, for instance, you can't be president. Even if you came to America when you were a day old, you still are not eligible.

Third, in order to be president, you have to have lived in the United States for more than fourteen years.

★

So I have to wait a long time before I can run for political office.

Not as long as you think. When you turn thirty, you can be a state senator (if you're a citizen who has lived in the United States for nine years). And when you are just twenty-five, you can be a representative (if you're a citizen who has lived in the United States for seven years). In both cases, you have to be a resident of the state that elects you.

★

My mom and dad meet the qualifications for president. Can they run?

Yes, but they probably won't unless your mom or dad is a member of Congress or the governor of a state. Most people who decide to run for president are well-known politicians who have worked in government for a long time. Voters want the leader of our country to be a person who has won previous elections, has a lot of experience, and has already proven he can manage people and put ideas into action.

★

Can a person who is not a politician become president?

Yes. George Washington was a soldier and a farmer before he was elected president of the United States. He never even went to college.

But in the twentieth century, the only American president who had not been a politician before was Dwight Eisenhower.

Eisenhower was an American general and the commander of the Allied forces in Europe during World War II. When the war was over, he retired and was appointed president of Columbia University.

Both the Democrats and Republicans asked "Ike" to be their presidential nominee in 1948. But he said a soldier should not be president. They kept asking, and in 1952 Eisenhower agreed to run as a Republican. He won, and also won a second term in 1956.

Many other nonpoliticians have run for president, but haven't won. In 1940, the Republicans nominated Wendell Willkie, a businessman who had no political experience. Dr. Benjamin Spock, the world-famous pediatrician, ran for president in 1972. He got 77,080 votes.

In 1968, Dick Gregory and Pat Paulsen, two comedians, ran for president. Paulsen's campaign was strictly a joke. But Gregory's was quite serious, and 47,097 people cast their votes for him. And in 2012, Herman Cain ran for president. Before that, he was most well known for being the chairman and CEO of the Godfather's Pizza chain.

★

Can you run for president if you're in jail?

No.

★

Why don't we just pick the smartest person in the United States to be president?

Two reasons. First, "smart" is hard to measure. Who is to say who the smartest person in the United States is? If you use IQ tests, you will find lots of people who are geniuses.

Second, just because somebody is a genius does not mean that person would make a good president. Besides being smart, the president must be a good leader, a good communicator, have good instincts, work well with people, and be liked by the public. There are lots of smart people in this country, but only a very few capable of leading the country.

★

Why do people want to be president so badly?

There are several reasons. We would hope that candidates run for president because they want to serve their country and honestly believe they can accomplish great things in that job that will make the world a better place for everyone.

A candidate may also feel they have a calling. In other words, they may feel they were *meant* to be president and the nation needs them to be its leader. George Washington probably felt that way when the country was founded. Some candidates may run for president because they want to be a part of history.

Finally, let's admit it, some people probably run for president simply because it's the most powerful position in the world. It's the highest you can go.

If you're a skater, you want to win the Olympic gold medal. If you're a movie director, you want to win the Academy Award for Best Picture. And if you're a politician, you just might want to be president of the United States.

★

What are the qualifications to be vice president?

The qualifications for vice president are the same as those for president: You must be thirty-five years old, born in the United States, and have lived in the United States for fourteen years.

★

How is the vice president selected?

Up until 1804, the vice president was simply the person who came in second in the presidential election. That system didn't work very well, because frequently the top two vote-getters were rivals who did not get along well.

These days, the candidate for vice president is usually chosen by the presidential candidate before the national convention. That person is called a "running mate."

★

What would make a candidate select a particular person as a running mate?

Interestingly, candidates for president usually pick running mates who are *different* from themselves. If one is from the eastern part of the country, chances are the other will be from a western state. If one is from the north, the other is often from a southern state. If one is slightly left (liberal), the other might be slightly right (conservative). If one is old, the other might be young. This is called "balancing the ticket."

They do it this way for one reason: to get the highest possible number of votes. Voters in Texas might not want to vote for a presidential candidate who comes from Massachusetts. So the candidate may select a prominent Texan as his running mate (as Kennedy selected Johnson in 1960) because people in Texas will probably vote for him even if they don't like him.

The candidate wants to choose a running mate who will attract voters who wouldn't otherwise vote for that candidate.

Of course, the candidate also looks for a running mate he can work with, who will help accomplish his goals, and who can carry out the responsibilities of the vice presidential office.

★

What are the vice president's responsibilities?

Up until around World War II, the vice president's main job was to hang around in case the president died and someone was needed to take his place. Indeed, the vice president is "only a heartbeat away" from being president of the United States, and that in itself is a very important responsibility.

John Adams was the nation's first vice president, or "veep." He called the job "the most insignificant" in the world. But he also said, "In this I am nothing. But I could be everything."

In the Constitution, the vice president has only one responsibility: to preside over the Senate. If the one hundred senators vote fifty-fifty on an issue, the vice president casts the deciding vote.

Over the years, as the president's job became more complicated and demanding, vice presidents have taken on more responsibility. In 1921 they began attending cabinet meetings. In 1949 they became members of the National Security Council. These days the vice president works almost hand in hand with the president, helping set policy, attending important meetings, and taking the place of the president at official functions. It is no longer a meaningless position.

★

Can a candidate quit in the middle of the campaign?

Fortunately, yes. If none of the many candidates for president ever quit, the election process would be even more complicated than it is already.

Some candidates drop out of the race because they don't have enough money to continue campaigning. Others drop out if the polls suggest they have no chance of winning. Occasionally a candidate will drop out because of a scandal, or because the press has discovered something about their personal life that might prevent people from voting for them.

★

Can a candidate run for president more than once?

Sure. Richard Nixon lost the presidential election in 1960, then came back and won it in 1968 and 1972. Four other presidents lost before they won (John Quincy Adams, Andrew Jackson, William Henry Harrison, and Grover Cleveland).

There have been some lesser candidates who have run for president repeatedly without winning. Eric Hass of the Socialist Labor Party ran for president in 1952, 1956, 1960, and 1964. The most votes he ever got in one election was 48,000.

The all-time record for running for president goes to Harold Stassen, a Republican from Minnesota. He first ran for president in 1948. He didn't get many votes, but he must have enjoyed the experience, because he ran for president *eight* more times until he lost his final election in 1992.

★

Do the candidates hate each other?

Some do, some don't. In the heat of a political campaign, angry words are sometimes exchanged. Tempers flare. Candidates often accuse their opponent of spreading lies about them or their record. People with very different positions on important issues may despise each other.

But very often, candidates who oppose one another have also worked with each other for many years in Congress or as state governors and genuinely like and respect each other. It is not at all unusual for a liberal and a conservative to be friends "out of the office."

When one candidate defeats another for their party's nomination or for the presidency, the loser always congratulates the winner and wishes him luck. Even if they do hate each other, both candidates hope the nation will unite behind the winner and lead the nation in the right direction.

★

Do candidates write their own speeches?

Abraham Lincoln, the story goes, wrote his famous Gettysburg Address on the back of an envelope. But even back in Lincoln's day, politicians were using speechwriters. Lincoln's first inaugural address was written by William Seward, his secretary of state.

Speeches by presidents and candidates often touch on many different issues and can run an hour or longer. Few candidates have the time to write every word of every speech. Professional speechwriters usually write the first draft. The candidate then looks it over carefully and edits it, making additions, cuts, and changes.

Sometimes a speechwriter will create a phrase that enters the language. Peggy Noonan, a speechwriter for Presidents Reagan and Bush, became famous for writing the "thousand points of light" speech that George Bush delivered to accept the 1988 Republican nomination for president.

★

★ ★ ★ ★ ★ ★ ★ ★ ★ ★ ★ ★ ★ ★ ★ ★

CHAPTER 5

Voting

Why is voting important?

In a nation of more than 300 million people, it may seem like voting really isn't that important. With so many other people out there voting, what difference could one vote for or against a candidate mean?

In fact, it could make a lot of difference. Consider this: In the 1882 election to the Virginia House of Representatives, this is the way the voting turned out:

Robert Mayo: 10,505

George Garrison: 10,504

If just *one* voter had cast a ballot for Garrison instead of Mayo, Garrison and Mayo would have tied, and the election would have had to happen all over again. And that wasn't a once-in-a-lifetime event. Four times in American history, federal elections were decided by a single vote.

Also consider this: One vote saved President Andrew Johnson from being removed from office in 1868. One vote gave Adolf Hitler the leadership of Germany's Nazi Party in 1923.

Each vote counts. In some other countries, citizens cannot vote or have a say in the way their government is run. Millions of people come to America for the simple reason that we have the right to vote. That right should not be taken for granted.

By voting, we can change laws we disagree with. We can "fire" leaders who we feel are not doing a good job. Our democracy only reflects what Americans want if Americans vote.

★

When can I vote for President?

The day you turn eighteen years old, you become a legal adult. Then you will be old enough to vote in any election.

ELECTION!

THE CONSTITUTION (Amendment XXVI, Section I): "The right of citizens of the United States, who are eighteen years of age or older, to vote shall not be denied or abridged by the United States or by any State on account of age."

★

Can I just show up on Election Day once I turn eighteen?

No. First you have to register to vote in the community where you live. This may have to be done well in advance of Election Day, depending on your state.

★

How do I register to vote?

It is pretty simple and only takes a few minutes. You just go to the voter registration office at your local city hall and ask for a voter registration card. After you fill it out and send it in, you will receive a notice in the mail telling you where you go to vote. If you move to another town or state, you have to register to vote again.

★

Are there any grown-ups who aren't allowed to vote?

Yes. People who are not American citizens cannot vote. Neither can citizens who aren't registered, temporary visitors, convicted criminals, or the insane. Also, each state has its own residency requirement. You have to live in your state for a minimum amount of time before you can vote there.

But we're talking about very small numbers of people here. Almost all Americans have the right to vote.

★

Has it always been that way?

No. When America was in its infancy, very *few* people were allowed to vote. Different states had different requirements, but in general:

Before 1825, people who didn't own land could not vote.

Before 1870, African Americans could not vote.

Before 1920, women could not vote. (Spain gave

women the vote in 1931. Italy and France waited until after World War II. Women in Switzerland couldn't vote until 1971.)

Before 1924, Native Americans could not vote.

Before 1964, people who lived in Washington, D.C., could not vote (for president).

Before 1971, eighteen- to twenty-year-olds could not vote. (During the Vietnam War, many Americans felt it wasn't fair that teenagers could be drafted to fight and die for their country while they were not allowed to vote. The Twenty-sixth Amendment lowered the voting age to eighteen.)

Even after these various groups were given the right to vote, in many cases the system made it difficult for them. They had to pass literacy tests, learn to speak English, or travel long distances. It took several Voting Rights Acts of the 1960s and 1970s to eliminate the barriers to fair registration and voting for all.

In 1993, Congress passed what came to be called the "motor-voter" bill: Citizens can register to vote when they apply for a driver's license.

★

Can they vote in Puerto Rico, the Virgin Islands, and Guam?

Puerto Rico, the Virgin Islands, and Guam are territories of the United States, but citizens there cannot vote for president.

★

Where do you go to vote?

The "polling place" in your neighborhood may be your church, a local firehouse, or even your school.

If you go with a parent on Election Day, you will see signs outside the polling place saying it is against the law to campaign there. Inside, there will be a bunch of election officials, volunteers, and one or more voting machines. Your parent will wait in line, then give their name to an election official. That person will check in a book to make sure your parent is registered to vote. They will check off the name to make sure nobody tries to vote twice (it happens!). Then your parent will be told which voting machine to use.

★

How does a voting machine work?

In ancient Greece, the citizens voted simply by raising their hand. That wasn't exactly fair, though. If everybody knew how you were going to vote, people could pressure you to vote a certain way and make sure you did what they told you.

What was needed was a "secret ballot." This is sometimes called an "Australian ballot" because it was developed there in the 1850s.

In early America, they used wooden ballot boxes with a slot at the top to slip in a piece of paper that had been marked for one candidate or another. There were problems there, too. It took a long time to count all those slips of paper. Sometimes there were mistakes. Sometimes election officials were bribed to make "mistakes."

The first voting machines were used in Lockport, New York, in 1892. They've changed quite a bit since then, but the basic idea is still the same. Here's how a voting machine works.

You step into a large booth about the size of

a bathroom stall. You pull a switch that closes a curtain behind you so nobody can see who you're voting for. The switch also "unlocks" the voting machine so votes can be cast. In front of you is a list of candidates and the positions they are running for. The presidency is probably not the only job up for grabs. People may be running for governor of the state, senator, mayor, sheriff, judge, and so on.

Next to each name is a button or a small lever that can be flipped, like a light switch. You flip the levers next to the names of the candidates you want to vote for. The machine has been set up so that you can only vote for *one* person for each political opening. You can, however, change your mind after you flip a lever and flip it back. But most people know who they're going to vote for when they enter the booth.

If you're satisfied with your selections, you pull the switch again. This opens the curtain and automatically adds your vote to all the others that have been cast on that machine.

★

ELECTION!

Can I go into the booth with my mom or dad?

Give it a shot. Some election officials will appreciate
your interest in the democratic process. Others will say
you can't go in the booth if you're not a registered voter.
If you do go in, let your mom or dad pull the levers.

★

What happens after that?

When the polls close at the end of the day, an election
judge will lock up the voting machine so no more votes
can be cast on it. (They'll keep it locked for thirty days
in case a recount needs to be done.) A compartment
on the machine is opened in front of several witnesses.
The results are recorded. The election judge prepares
a certificate showing how the vote came out. This is
given to the board of elections, which compiles the
results from all the voting machines in that district
and reports the results.

There has been talk that someday elections will be
done entirely online. We can sit in the comfort of our
homes, vote via the Internet, and get the results from
the entire country in seconds. For now, we still use

voting machines. In fact, in some parts of the nation, they still use paper ballots.

★

Do you have to vote for your political party's candidate if you don't like that person?

No. Lots of Democrats will vote for the Republican candidate, and lots of Republicans will vote for the Democratic candidate. This is called "crossing party lines," and there's nothing wrong with it.

Each political party can count on a certain number of its members ("faithfuls") to vote for that party no matter who their candidate is. But a very large number of Americans, possibly as high as one-third, don't make their decision until just before Election Day. These "undecideds" are very important. The candidate who can convince them to give him their vote is very often the one who will win the election.

★

If I was eligible to vote, could I vote for my teacher instead of the candidates?

Yes. At the polling place, they have what are called "irregular ballots" for people who wish to write in the name of someone who is not on the ballot. There are always a few jokers who write in names like "Mickey Mouse" as a protest against the election process. But almost all voters vote for one of the candidates who is running.

★

Can you vote if you're out of town on Election Day?

Yes. Some people can't make it to the polls. This would include people who are in the hospital or disabled, people on vacation, college students living away from home, people in the military, and people on business trips.

In those cases, citizens can vote if they get an "absentee ballot." It's simply a form that is filled out and must be mailed to the local board of elections in advance of Election Day so it can be counted.

★

Does everybody vote who is registered to vote?

Sadly, no. In the 1960 presidential election, less than 63 percent of all the registered voters actually voted. If you think that's low, in the 1996 presidential election, only 49 percent voted. For the first time in American history, less than half the registered voters made the effort to vote.

Some groups tend to vote more than others. Wealthy people vote more than poor people do. Educated people vote more than uneducated people do. Older people vote more than younger people do. The lowest voter "turnout" is among the eighteen- to twenty-one-year-olds.

In other democracies such as Japan, Italy, and Australia, voter turnout is much higher than it is in the United States. But then, in Australia, citizens who don't vote are actually *fined*.

★

Why would anyone not vote?

There are a lot of reasons. Some people simply have a hard time getting to the polls. (See above: Can you vote if you're out of town on Election Day?) Others are simply too lazy, or the opposite—too busy to take time from their job.

Some people are satisfied with the way things are going and don't see any need to vote for a change. Some are completely disinterested and just figure that people who care more than they do will make good decisions for the country. Still others say they haven't paid close attention to the issues, so they don't feel they can make an informed choice among the candidates.

Finally, some people complain that they don't like *any* of the candidates, or they are so disillusioned with politics that they feel it wouldn't matter which candidates were running the country, anyway.

And sometimes it rains on Election Day and people don't want to go outside.

There are lots of reasons people give not to vote, but there aren't any *good* reasons. Everybody who is eligible to vote should vote. Democracy shouldn't be taken for granted.

(See the beginning of this chapter: Why is voting important?)

★

How do people decide which candidate to vote for?

Each voter has his or her own reason for voting for a particular candidate. Voters examine the candidate's record of what they've accomplished; decide if the candidate shares their values; determine if the candidate is smart, honest, and a good leader. A voter will look over the issues (foreign policy, domestic policy, taxes, the environment, and so on) to see where the candidates "stand" on each one.

Some people vote for whomever their political party nominates, figuring that if they agree with the party's positions, so will the party's candidate. Other people have one particular issue that is important to them, and whichever candidate shares their opinion on that issue will get their vote. Still others vote "with their pocketbooks." In other words, if the economy is good, the political party that is currently in the majority (in Congress) will get their vote. If the news is bad, many voters will pull the lever for the minority party in hopes that they might run things differently.

A few factors that voters should *not* use to determine where to cast their vote are the candidate's skin color, gender, physical appearance, or what their spouse looks like. The fact that one candidate has cooler posters or bumper stickers should not affect anyone's choice.

Remember, the election is not a popularity contest. We are trying to choose the best person to lead the country for the next four years.

★

CHAPTER 6

★ ★ ★ ★ ★ ★ ★ ★ ★ ★ ★ ★ ★ ★ ★ ★ ★

The Election

When is Election Day?

Finally all the hoopla about the campaign is over, and it's time to make the big decision about who will be the nation's next president. Election Day is always the first Tuesday following the first Monday in November. In many states, schools, banks, and post offices are closed on that day.

★

Why was that day chosen for Election Day?

The decision was made back in 1845, when most Americans worked on farms. November was cho-

sen because the fall harvest should have been com-
pleted by then. The hard weather of winter hadn't
hit yet, so people were still able to travel long distances on the roads (usually unpaved) to get to the
polling place.

Tuesday was chosen because it might take a whole
day to get to the polling place, and if Election Day was
on Monday, people would have to leave on Sunday and
miss church.

If a local elected leader resigns or dies, a "special
election" may be held to choose a successor. But for
more than 150 years, Americans have voted for president on the first Tuesday following the first Monday in
November.

★

How long are the polls open?

It depends on where you live. In most states, the polls
open at six or seven o'clock in the morning. They close
that evening at six o'clock in Indiana, Kentucky, and
Hawaii (to name three), and at nine o'clock in Iowa,
New York, and Rhode Island.

Because the continental United States covers five

time zones, voting results on the East Coast come in before the West Coast. When it's dinnertime in New York, it's still midafternoon in California. Some years the TV networks have predicted the winner of the election before many people on the West Coast had even voted yet.

★

How can they predict the winner in advance?

All throughout Election Day, the TV networks and major news organizations race to predict the outcome of the election. They do it by taking what are called "exit polls." Basically, they ask people leaving polling places which candidate they voted for.

Obviously they can't ask everybody in the whole country who they voted for. But they can ask a small sample of voters in specific parts of each state. This is called "sampling."

Let's say there's a town called Anytown. A news organization might do an exit poll of a hundred people in Anytown and find out that sixty of them voted for the Republican candidate and forty voted for the Democratic candidate. The news organization assumes that if those hundred residents of Anytown are voting sixty-forty in favor of the Republican, the rest of Anytown will probably be voting that way, too.

The Anytown data is fed into computers. The computers have data from previous elections stored inside them. By analyzing the way Anytown voted in the past and the way it seems to be voting today, the news organization may be able to predict with confidence which candidate is going to get the most votes in Anytown. They may also be able to make predictions about other areas as well.

After you finish dinner on Election Day, turn on the TV, radio, or computer. All the major networks will be covering the election. Results will be trickling in from all over the country. Computers will be furiously crunching numbers. Commentators will be looking for trends, trying to figure out what the "early returns" indicate. Is the south going for one candidate? Is a candidate doing better or worse than the most recent polls would have led people to believe?

You'll see mounting tallies of votes in each state. At first they'll only have 1 percent of the vote counted.

Then 3 percent, then 5 percent. Soon the networks will start to declare winners. "In the state of Nebraska," they will say, "with five percent of the vote in, we project John Doe the winner."

★

Do they ever get it wrong?

Rarely. In 1948 all the polls had predicted a big victory for Thomas E. Dewey, the governor of New York. On Election Day, everyone was so sure that Dewey was going to win that the *Chicago Daily Tribune* printed an edition with the huge headline "DEWEY DEFEATS TRUMAN."

Well, when all the votes had been counted, Harry Truman won the election. There is a very famous photo of Truman holding up the front page of the newspaper with that incorrect headline.

Of course, that was before computers made it possible to analyze election results much more scientifically.

★

Do they always predict the winner so fast?

Not until recent elections. Back in 1916, Charles Evans Hughes was challenging President Woodrow Wilson. Hughes was ahead in the early voting, but not by much. The election came down to how California voted. The two candidates were neck and neck, and it wasn't until two days later that all the votes were counted. Wilson won the state of California by just four thousand votes, and won the election.

★

What difference does it make how one state votes? Isn't it the grand total of all the votes that matters?

This may come as a shock to you, but the answer is no. The total of all the votes— which is called the "popular vote"—does not determine the winner of the presidential election.

It all started, as many of our traditions do, with the Founding Fathers. As educated and fair-minded as they were, they did not feel that ordinary people were capable of choosing the president wisely.

To be fair to the Founding Fathers, many Americans could not read in the 1700s, and there was no radio, TV, or Internet to keep the public informed. Communication was slow. It took three days just to travel the ninety miles from New York City to Philadelphia.

In any case, they devised a system for electing the president that was based on the vote of the "electoral college" and not the popular vote.

☆

Electoral college? Isn't that where you go to learn how to be an electrician?

No. You'd better sit down for this. Lock yourself in a room and don't do any texting for a few minutes.

Each of our fifty states has a certain number of "electoral" votes equal to its number of senators and representatives. For example, California has two senators and fifty-three members of the House of Representatives. So California has fifty-five electoral votes (the most in the country).

Wyoming, on the other hand, only has three electoral votes, because they have a much smaller population. Wyoming has two senators, like every other state, but only one member of the House of Representatives.

Densely populated states (New York, Texas, Illinois, Michigan, Pennsylvania, Ohio) have large numbers of electoral votes, and less populated states (Alaska, Delaware, Hawaii, Idaho, Nevada, Vermont, North Dakota) have just a few electoral votes. Altogether, the country has 538 electoral votes.

On Election Day, the popular vote is tallied for each state. Whichever candidate wins the popular vote in each state wins all the electoral votes in that state. So whether candidate Doe wins the state of California by a single vote or a million votes, he wins all of California's fifty-five electoral votes.

To win the presidency, a candidate has to win a majority of the electoral votes. So when a candidate has won 270 electoral votes, he is the winner.

★

So what's the "college" in electoral college?

About a month after Election Day, "electors" will meet in all the state capitols. There is one elector for each of the 538 electoral votes. These electors are pledged to vote for the candidate who won the popular vote in that state. They cast electoral votes on behalf of the people of their state and officially elect the president. Collectively, these electors are called "the electoral college."

★

What's the point of that if everybody knew the electoral vote totals on Election Night?

It's a formality. In other words, it's something that is done even though it's not necessary.

The tradition goes back to the early days of this country, when the leaders did not feel the common man (women were not even considered) could choose the president. They felt that a few educated men should make this important decision. The system was originally set up so the people would vote for their state representatives, those representatives would select electors, and the electors would vote to determine the president.

The Founding Fathers did not know that political parties would spring up to choose candidates.

They had no idea that two hundred years later the people would be narrowing down the list of candidates through primary elections. (See Chapter 3: The Campaign.) The system is actually much fairer today, because millions of average Americans make the decision instead of a few people.

Everybody knows who wins the election on Election Night. But still, for the sake of tradition, the electoral college gathers in December to officially elect the president.

The electoral college system is not perfect. There have been many efforts over the years to change it or to get rid of it entirely. But the one thing going for the electoral college is that it has worked pretty well for more than two hundred years. And, as we say in America, "If it ain't broke, don't fix it."

★

Why don't they just add up all the votes, and whichever candidate has the most wins the election?

That would certainly be simpler. But it wouldn't necessarily be more fair.

Think about this: If the candidate with the most popular votes won the election, candidates would only campaign in areas that have a lot of people— major cities. If you could win the people in those cities, you could probably win the election even if most of the rest of the country voted against you. Similarly, the president in office would do all he could to favor the more populated areas, because the areas with fewer people wouldn't matter very much.

With the electoral college system, even the states with the fewest people have a minimum of three electoral votes (because each state has two senators and at least one representative). Thirty-one of our fifty states have nine electoral votes or less. If you add all their electoral votes together, it comes to 167. That's a big chunk of votes.

Candidates still spend most of their time campaigning in places that have the most people. But thanks to the electoral college, they cannot ignore the smaller states.

★

But isn't it possible to get the most popular votes and lose the election?

Yes. If a candidate were to win a few of the bigger states by just a few votes but lose badly in most of the smaller states, it would be possible to get the most popular votes and still not win the election.

In fact, it has happened four times. John Quincy Adams (1824), Rutherford B. Hayes (1876), and Benjamin Harrison (1888) all won the presidency even though they lost the popular vote. In 2001, Al Gore won the popular vote, but George W. Bush became the president.

★

What if none of the candidates wins a majority of the electoral votes?

If this happens, according to Article II, Section I, of the Constitution, the House of Representatives will select the president. Each state will cast one vote for one of the candidates who had the top three popular vote totals. The candidate with the majority of votes wins.

This has happened twice, with Thomas Jefferson in 1800 and John Quincy Adams in 1824.

In that 1824 election, it was a four-way race. Andrew Jackson won the popular vote, but not a majority of the electoral votes. The House of Representatives met, and Adams was elected president. If a third-party candidate were to win some big states, this could very well happen again.

★

What is a landslide?

A landslide is an election in which one candidate beats the other by a wide margin. In 1936, Franklin D. Roosevelt won 523 electoral votes, while Alf Landon won eight. *That* was a landslide!

A few other landslides in American history were:

Lincoln (212) over McClellan (21) in 1864.
Wilson (435) over Theodore Roosevelt (88) in
    1912.
Nixon (520) over McGovern (17) in 1972.
Reagan (523) over Mondale (13) in 1984.

When there is a landslide, the winner can reasonably conclude that he has been given a "mandate" by the American people. A mandate is a command to act in a particular way.

For instance, say candidate A campaigned heavily on the issue of free bicycles for everyone. His opponent was against giving out free bicycles. If candidate A wins the election in a landslide, he should expect Congress to pass a law giving bicycles to everyone. By voting him into office, the American people have said they agree with his policies. They have given him a mandate.

In a very close election, on the other hand, the winner will have to work harder to get his ideas accepted. He does not have a mandate.

★

What was the closest election in American history?

In the 1960 election, 69 million people voted. John F. Kennedy won the election, but he had only about 118,500 more votes than Richard Nixon. The popular vote totals were:

Kennedy: 34,227,096
Nixon: 34,108,546

In that election, Kennedy won only twenty-two states, but they were larger states so he won the electoral vote total 303 to 219.

Another very close election took place in 2000. Al Gore and George W. Bush were separated by about a half a million votes. In the end, it took the Supreme Court to decide the election.

★

Which president got more votes than any other?

Barack Obama. In 2008, he got more than 65 million votes.

★

What arc coattails?

As mentioned earlier, on Election Day people vote for many other offices in addition to president. Your governor, mayor, senator, and representative may be up for reelection, too. So voters have to pull a lot of levers in that voting booth.

Many people will pull the lever for the presidential candidate of their choice, and then vote for the other candidates in the same political party. When those candidates win their elections, it is said that they got in "on the coattails" of the president. In other words, they won their elections at least partially with the help and popularity of the president.

★

Does the political party that wins the presidency rule the country?

No. For one thing, no party rules the country. There is a "majority party" (the party that currently has the most seats in the House of Representatives) and a "minority party" (the party that has fewer seats). When they vote on an issue, clearly the majority party has an advantage. But the Democrats don't all vote the same way, and neither do all the Republicans.

For another thing, it is not at all uncommon for the president to be a member of one political party while Congress is controlled by the other party. This sometimes makes it difficult for the president to get his ideas, appointments, and policies approved. The more popular a president is with the people, the easier it will be for him to get his way with the Congress.

★

Does the best candidate always win?

Probably not. The best team doesn't win every game. The best actor doesn't always win the Academy Award. The best musician doesn't always have the most fans. Life isn't always fair.

There's really no way to tell who was the best candidate for president. We only get a chance to see the winner in office for those four years. We'll never know how things might have gone differently if the other candidate had won.

Each political party tries to narrow down the list of candidates to one who was capable of leading the country. If so, even if the best candidate doesn't win, the United States is in capable hands.

★

What is a concession speech?

This is a speech given by a candidate on Election Night when he realizes he has lost the election. It is usually given at his campaign headquarters before the people who worked hard on his behalf. He will thank them for

---

their efforts, and he will also send good luck wishes to the winner.

★

When does the new president take office?

At noon on January 20, a little more than two months after Election Day. This is the traditional day of the president's inauguration.

★

What is an inauguration?

This is the ceremony in which the new president takes the oath of office and officially begins his term. Except for a few unusual cases, the inauguration takes place outdoors, in front of the Capitol Building, in Washington, D.C. (Theodore Roosevelt was inaugurated in Buffalo, New York, after President McKinley died, and Lyndon Johnson was inaugurated on an airplane in Dallas, Texas, after President Kennedy died.)

Thousands of people come and fill the Mall that stretches from the Capitol to the Lincoln Memorial.

There are red, white, and blue flags and decorations everywhere.

The former president is in attendance. Even if he lost the election to the new president, he accepts the decision of the people. There has never been a transition from one president to the next that did not go smoothly.

At noon, the chief justice of the Supreme Court leads the new president through the oath of office:

"I do solemnly swear that I will faithfully execute the Office of President of the United States, and will to the best of my Ability, preserve, protect and defend the Constitution of the United States."

The new president then gives an inaugural speech and parades down Pennsylvania Avenue to the White House. That evening, he and his wife attend a series of inaugural balls.

★

Can kids influence an election even though they can't vote?

Absolutely. The leaders of our nation represent all of us, even those who can't vote yet. They make decisions that affect you. You have every right to make your voice heard.

If you want to influence the election, the first thing you need to do is to decide which candidate to support. Read the newspapers. Watch the debates. Check out the Web sites at the end of this book. Ask questions. Learn everything you can about the candidates so you can make a good decision. See where they stand on the issues you consider important. Try to look beyond the TV commercials, slogans, songs, and campaign hoopla.

Once you form an opinion and decide to help one of the candidates, there is a lot you can do. You can volunteer time at the local campaign headquarters to pass out flyers, answer phones, or lick and address envelopes.

On Election Day you can help elderly or handicapped people you know get to the polls to vote. You can baby-sit for parents to make it easier for them to get out of the house and vote.

After the election is over, don't stop caring. If you feel strongly about something, write a letter to the president (1600 Pennsylvania Avenue, Washington, D.C. 20500). The president might even write you back.

You can also write to your senators (United States Senate, Washington, D.C. 20510) or representative (United States House of Representatives, Washington, D.C. 20510).

Remember that the United States was founded by people who believed in a cause and fought for it. Laws have been changed by people who believed in a cause and fought for it. That's how slavery and segregation ended, how women got the vote, how the drinking age was raised to twenty-one, and the voting age lowered to eighteen. Americans fighting for change brought an end to a war and even drove a president from office.

Our nation's leaders pay very close attention to what the public thinks. You are the public, too. In just a few years, you will be voting. But until then, you are never too young to make a difference in the way our government is run.

★

Words You'll Hear in an Election Year

* * *

ballot: Something, such as a piece of paper, with the names of the candidates in an election. The voter marks his choice with a pencil or, if a voting machine is used, pulls a lever next to the candidate's name.

bandwagon: the side in an election that seems most likely to win. Voters are said to "jump on the bandwagon."

benefit: an event to raise money for a candidate or a cause

bill: a proposed law to be voted on by Congress

Bill of Rights: the first ten amendments to the Constitution of the United States, which protect our basic rights, such as freedom of speech and religion

cabinet: the heads of the fourteen governmental departments, appointed by the president, who meet regularly with him and give him advice

campaign: a series of planned actions for accomplishing a goal, such as getting a candidate elected

candidate: a person who runs for office chief justice: the judge who is head of the Supreme Court

compromise: a settlement to a dispute in which each side gives up something

Congress: The group of elected officials in the United States government who make up the legislative branch. It consists of the House of Representatives and the Senate.

contribution: money or other aid given for a candidate or cause

dark horse: a candidate who is not well-known and seems to have little chance of winning an election

debate: a formal discussion in which candidates give opinions and argue over issues

delegate: a person chosen to act or speak on behalf of a group

democracy: a form of government where the people hold the ruling power, usually giving it over to representatives whom they elect

Democratic Party: one of the two main political parties in the United States

electoral college: the group of people who elect the president of the United States, based on the votes of the people in their states

endorsement: to give support to a candidate or cause

executive branch: the branch of government headed by the president of the United States

grass roots: Having to do with the common person. A grass roots campaign uses the help of many citizen volunteers.

impeach: the process of bringing charges against a person in office

inauguration: the ceremony where the president is sworn into office

independent voter: a voter who is not a member of a political party *issues:* problems and concerns that are talked over by candidates

judicial branch: the branch of the United States government headed by the Supreme Court

legislative branch: the Congress of the United States, which makes laws; Congress is divided into the House of Representatives and the Senate

party: an organized group of people who share the same political opinions and try to get a candidate elected

patronage: favors given out by public officials, such as offices and honors

platform: a political party's statement of its stand on important issues

political: having to do with government and politics

political parties: organizations, such as the Democrats and Republicans, that work to get their candidates elected to public office

polling place: the place where people go to vote

poll: a record of people's opinions on a particular subject

primary election: a special election held to choose the candidates for the final election

registration: To record a person's name on a state's official list of those entitled to vote. In every state, a person must register in order to vote.

representative democracy: a form of government where citizens elect officials to govern them

Republican Party: one of the two main political parties in the United States

separation of powers: the system of government in the United States where the three branches of government (executive, legislative, and judicial) have different powers to make sure that one branch does not have too much control

stumping: to travel around making campaign speeches

term: the length of time an elected official is in office

third party: any political party other than the two main political parties in the United States *unconstitutional:* a law or action that a national court has decided violates the Constitution

veto: the procedure that allows the president of the United States to turn down a bill passed by Congress

Find Out More!

* * *

Buller, Jon. *Smart About the Presidents*, Grosset & Dunlap, 2004.

Davis, Christopher. *I Wish I Knew That: U.S. Presidents: Cool Stuff You Need To Know,* Reader's Digest Juvenile, 2012.

Blassingame, Wyatt. *The Look-It-Up Book of Presidents,* Random House Books for Young Readers, 1990.

Thornton, Brian. *The Everything Kids' Presidents Book,* Adams Media, 2007.

The Internet is filled with hundreds of sites with information about the presidency, our government, politics, elections, and voting. In fact, much of the information in this book was gathered from online sources.

A great place to start is the League of Women Voters. Their address on the Web is www.lwv.org. There are also links to dozens of other sites.

Or, if you prefer, you might want to visit some of these sites:

The White House: http://www.whitehouse.gov

The Republican Party: http://www.gop.com

The Democratic Party: http://www.democrats.org/

The Federal Election Commission: http://www.fec.gov/

Public Agenda Online: http://www.publicagenda.org/

Rock the Vote: http://www.rockthevote.org/

Project Vote Smart: http://www.vote-smart.org/

United States Department of Justice: http://www.usdoj.gov/

Presidents of
the United States

★ ★ ★

Name: George Washington

Party: Federalist

Date of Birth: Feb. 22, 1732

Place of Birth: Westmoreland County, VA

Term: 1989–1797

Date of Death: Dec. 14, 1799

Place of Death: Mount Vernon, VA

Name: John Adams

Party: Federalist

Date of Birth: Oct. 30, 1735

Place of Birth: Braintree, MA

Term: 1797–1801

Date of Death: July 4, 1826

Place of Death: Quincy, MA

Name: Thomas Jefferson

Party: Democratic-Republican

Date of Birth: Apr. 13, 1743

Place of Birth: Albemarle County, VA

Term: 1801–1809

Date of Death: July 4, 1826

Place of Death: Charlottesville, VA

Name: James Madison

Party: Democratic-Republican

Date of Birth: Mar. 16, 1751

Place of Birth: Port Conway, VA

Term: 1809–1817

Date of Death: June 28, 1836

Place of Death: Orange County, VA

Name: James Monroe

Party: Democratic-Republican

Date of Birth: Apr. 28, 1785

Place of Birth: Westmoreland County, VA

Term: 1817–1825

Date of Death: July 4, 1831

Place of Death: New York, NY

Name: John Quincy Adams

Party: Democratic-Republican

Date of Birth: July 11, 1767

Place of Birth: Braintree, MA

Term: 1825–1829

Date of Death: Feb. 23, 1848

Place of Death: Washington, D.C.

Name: Andrew Jackson

Party: Democratic

Date of Birth: Mar. 15, 1767

Place of Birth: Waxhaw, SC

Term: 1829–1837

Date of Death: June 8, 1845

Place of Death: Nashville, TN

Name: Martin Van Buren

Party: Democratic

Date of Birth: Dec. 5, 1782

Place of Birth: Kinderhook, NY

Term: 1837–1841

Date of Death: July 24, 1862

Place of Death: Kinderhook, NY

Name: William H. Harrison

Party: Whig

Date of Birth: Feb. 9, 1773

Place of Birth: Berkeley, VA

Term: 1841

Date of Death: Apr. 4, 1841

Place of Death: Washington, D.C.

Name: John Tyler

Party: Whig

Date of Birth: Mar. 29, 1790

Place of Birth: Charles City County, VA

Term: 1841–1845

Date of Death: Jan. 18, 1862

Place of Death: Richmond, VA

Name: James K. Polk

Party: Democratic

Date of Birth: Nov. 2, 1795

Place of Birth: Mecklenburg County, NC

Term: 1845–1849

Date of Death: June 15, 1849

Place of Death: Nashville, TN

Name: Zachary Taylor

Party: Whig

Date of Birth: Nov. 24, 1784

Place of Birth: Orange County, VA

Term: 1849–1850

Date of Death: July 9, 1850

Place of Death: Washington, D.C.

Name: Millard Fillmore

Party: Whig

Date of Birth: Jan. 7, 1800

Place of Birth: Locke, NY

Term: 1850–1853

Date of Death: Mar. 8, 1874

Place of Death: Buffalo, NY

Name: Franklin Pierce

Party: Democratic

Date of Birth: Nov. 23, 1804

Place of Birth: Hillsborough County, NH

Term: 1853–1857

Date of Death: Oct. 8, 1869

Place of Death: Concord, NH

Name: James Buchanan

Party: Democratic

Date of Birth: Apr. 23, 1791

Place of Birth: Stony Batter, PA

Term: 1857–1861

Date of Death: June 1, 1868

Place of Death: Lancaster, PA

Name: Abraham Lincoln

Party: Republican

Date of Birth: Feb. 12, 1809

Place of Birth: Hardin County, KY

Term: 1861–1865

Date of Death: Apr. 15, 1865

Place of Death: Washington, D.C.

Name: Andrew Johnson

Party: Democratic

Date of Birth: Dec. 29, 1808

Place of Birth: Raleigh, NC

Term: 1865–1869

Date of Death: July 31, 1875

Place of Death: Carter Station, TN

Name: Ulysses S. Grant

Party: Republican

Date of Birth: Apr. 27, 1822

Place of Birth: Point Pleasant, OH

Term: 1869–1877

Date of Death: July 23, 1885

Place of Death: Mount McGregor, NY

Name: Rutherford B. Hayes

Party: Republican

Date of Birth: Oct. 4, 1822

Place of Birth: Delaware, OH

Term: 1877–1881

Date of Death: Jan. 17, 1893

Place of Death: Fremont, OH

Name: James A. Garfield

Party: Republican

Date of Birth: Nov. 19, 1831

Place of Birth: Orange, OH

Term: 1881

Date of Death: Sept. 19, 1881

Place of Death: Elberon, NJ

Name: Chester A. Arthur

Party: Republican

Date of Birth: Oct. 5, 1830

Place of Birth: Fairfield, VT

Term: 1881–1885

Date of Death: Nov. 18, 1886

Place of Death: New York, NY

Name: Grover Cleveland

Party: Democratic

Date of Birth: Mar. 18, 1837

Place of Birth: Caldwell, NJ

Term: 1885–1889, 1893–1897

Date of Death: June 24, 1908

Place of Death: Princeton, NJ

Name: Benjamin Harrison

Party: Republican

Date of Birth: Aug. 20, 1833

Place of Birth: North Bend, OH

Term: 1889–1893

Date of Death: Mar. 13, 1901

Place of Death: Indianapolis, IN

Name: William McKinley

Party: Republican

Date of Birth: Jan. 29, 1843

Place of Birth: Niles, OH

Term: 1897–1901

Date of Death: Sept. 14, 1901

Place of Death: Buffalo, NY

Name: Theodore Roosevelt

Party: Republican

Date of Birth: Oct. 27, 1858

Place of Birth: New York, NY

Term: 1901–1909

Date of Death: Jan. 6, 1919

Place of Death: Oyster Bay, NY

Name: William H. Taft

Party: Republican

Date of Birth: Sep. 15, 1857

Place of Birth: Cincinnati, OH

Term: 1909–1913

Date of Death: Mar. 8, 1931

Place of Death: Washington, D.C.

Name: Woodrow Wilson

Party: Democratic

Date of Birth: Dec. 28, 1856

Place of Birth: Staunton, VA

Term: 1913–1921

Date of Death: Feb. 3, 1924

Place of Death: Washington, D.C.

Name: Warren G. Harding

Party: Republican

Date of Birth: Nov. 2, 1865

Place of Birth: Corsica, OH

Term: 1921–1923

Date of Death: Aug. 2, 1923

Place of Death: San Francisco, CA

Name: Calvin Coolidge

Party: Republican

Date of Birth: July 4, 1872

Place of Birth: Plymouth Notch, VT

Term: 1923–1929

Date of Death: Jan. 5, 1933

Place of Death: Plymouth, VT

Name: Herbert Hoover

Party: Republican

Date of Birth: Aug. 10, 1874

Place of Birth: West Branch, IA

Term: 1929–1933

Date of Death: Oct. 20, 1964

Place of Death: New York, NY

Name: Franklin D. Roosevelt

Party: Democratic

Date of Birth: Jan. 30, 1882

Place of Birth: Hyde Park, NY

Term: 1933–1945

Date of Death: Apr. 12, 1945

Place of Death: Warm Springs, GA

Name: Harry S. Truman

Party: Democratic

Date of Birth: May 8, 1884

Place of Birth: Lamar, MO

Term: 1945–1953

Date of Death: Dec. 26, 1972

Place of Death: Kansas City, MO

Name: Dwight D. Eisenhower

Party: Republican

Date of Birth: Oct. 14, 1890

Place of Birth: Denison, TX

Term: 1953–1961

Date of Death: Mar. 28, 1969

Place of Death: Washington, D.C.

Name: John F. Kennedy

Party: Democratic

Date of Birth: May 29, 1917

Place of Birth: Brookline, MA

Term: 1961–1963

Date of Death: Nov. 22, 1963

Place of Death: Dallas, TX

Name: Lyndon B. Johnson

Party: Democratic

Date of Birth: Aug. 27, 1908

Place of Birth: Stonewall, TX

Term: 1963–1969

Date of Death: Jan. 22, 1973

Place of Death: San Antonio, TX

Name: Richard M. Nixon

Party: Republican

Date of Birth: Jan. 9, 1913

Place of Birth: Yorba Linda, CA

Term: 1969–1974

Date of Death: Apr. 22, 1994

Place of Death: New York, NY

Name: Gerald R. Ford

Party: Republican

Date of Birth: July 14, 1913

Place of Birth: Omaha, NE

Term: 1974–1977

Date of Death: N/A

Name: James Carter

Party: Democratic

Date of Birth: Oct. 1, 1924

Place of Birth: Plains, GA

Term: 1977–1981

Date of Death: N/A

Name: Ronald Reagan

Party: Republican

Date of Birth: Feb. 6, 1911

Place of Birth: Tampico, IL

Term: 1981–1989

Date of Death: N/A

Name: George Bush

Party: Republican

Date of Birth: June 12, 1924

Place of Birth: Milton, MA

Term: 1989–1993

Date of Death: N/A

Name: William Clinton

Party: Democratic

Date of Birth: Aug. 19, 1946

Place of Birth: Hope, AR

Term: 1993–2001

Date of Death: N/A

Name: George W. Bush

Party: Republican

Date of Birth: July 6, 1946

Place of Birth: New Haven, CT

Term: 2001–2009

Date of Death: N/A

Name: Barack Obama

Party: Democrat

Date of Birth: August 4, 1961

Place of Birth: Honolulu, HI

Term: 2009–

Date of Death: N/A

copyright © 2012 by Dan Gutman

cover design by Mimi Bark

ISBN 978-1-4532-7066-0

Published in 2012 by Open Road Integrated Media

180 Varick Street

New York, NY 10014

www.openroadmedia.com

INTEGRATED MEDIA

Videos, Archival Documents, and New Releases

Sign up for the Open Road Media newsletter and get news delivered straight to your inbox.

FOLLOW US:
@openroadmedia and
Facebook.com/OpenRoadMedia

SIGN UP NOW at
www.openroadmedia.com/newsletters

CPSIA information can be obtained at www.ICGtesting.com
Printed in the USA
BVOW010120120912

300098BV00002B/2/P